Earthquake Insurance: A Public Policy Dilemma

May 1985

Developed by the
Southern California Earthquake Preparedness Project

FEDERAL EMERGENCY MANAGEMENT AGENCY

Abstract

Title	Earthquake Insurance: A Public Policy Dilemma
Authors	The Southern California Earthquake Preparedness Project, James D. Goltz, Principal Researcher
Subject	Issues and recommendations regarding earthquake insurance for homeowners, businesses, local governments and special districts
Planning Agency	The Southern California Earthquake Preparedness Project
Number of Pages	48

Abstract

The purpose of this report is to examine issues and problems associated with the availability and procurement of earthquake insurance from points of view of both consumers and providers. The discussion outlines the provisions of earthquake insurance policies currently available to homeowners, businesses, local governments and special districts. It examines the extent to which earthquake insurance is purchased or why it may be unattractive to consumers. The Federal role in providing or promoting earthquake insurance is reviewed. Finally, policies are recommended for the Federal Government and others in order to develop a more adequate system of coverage.

Southern California Earthquake Preparedness Project
Policy Advisory Board
1983-84

The Southern California Earthquake Preparedness Project Policy Advisory Board guides the work of the Southern California Earthquake Preparedness Project and provides outreach to the planning communities.

Chairman   **Homer Givin**
Vice Chairman   **Robert Gibson**

Government

Cal McElwain	Supervisor, County of San Bernardino
* Deborah Barmack	Administrative Assistant to Supervisor Cal McElwain
Norton Younglove	Supervisor, County of Riverside
* Robert Horrigan	Emergency Services Director, County of Riverside
Evar Peterson	Councilman, City of Westminster
* Rafael Kenealy	Councilman, City of Chino
Ezunial Burts	Executive Assistant to the Mayor, City of Los Angeles

California Seismic Safety Commission

Richard Andrews	Executive Director
Robert Cheney	Commissioner

Structural Safety

Ted M. Christensen	Structural Engineers Association of Southern California
Eugene Zeller	Superintendent of Building and Safety, City of Long Beach
* Alexander Pyper	Superintendent of Buildings, City of Glendale

Earth Sciences/Prediction

James Davis	State Geologist, State of California
* Cliffton Gray, Jr.	California Division of Mines and Geology
Robert E. Wallace	United States Geological Survey
* David P. Hill	United States Geological Survey
Karen McNally	Earth Science Board, University of California, Santa Cruz
*Thomas Heaton	United States Geological Survey

Business and Industry

Homer Givin	Chairman, Seismic Safety Committee, IBM Corporation
Robert Gibson	President and CEO, Valley Federal Savings and Loan

Education

Joan Wertz	Director, Head Start Program, County of Los Angeles

* Denotes alternates

ii

Emergency Services

Walter T. Johnson, Jr. Southern California Emergency Services Association
* Anthony Prud'homme Director, Emergency Planning, Atlantic Richfield Company
Jack Kearns California State Office of Emergency Services
* James Alexander California State Office of Emergency Services

American Red Cross

James Haigwood Associate Manager
* Pat Snyder Volunteer Consultant

Federal Emergency Management Agency

Terrance Meade Community Planner
* Laurie Friedman Community Planner

Social Sciences

Henry Reining, Jr. Dean Emeritus, University of Southern California (USC)
* Robert Stallings Professor of Public Administration, USC

* Denotes alternates

Southern California Earthquake Preparedness Project

Paul J. Flores, Project Director

James D. Goltz, Principal Researcher

Gilbert V. Najera, Insurance Study Program Manager

Project Staff

Joan M. Arias, Education Program Supervisor

Paula Schulz, Planning Officer

Melanie C. Ingram, Program Analyst

Cheryl Tateishi, Planning Officer

Jeff Sampson, Education Officer

Greg Warnagieris, Education Officer

Michelle Banford, Office Technician

Nesta McAteer, Office Technician

Acknowledgments

The Southern California Earthquake Preparedness Project is indebted to numerous people who contributed to the earthquake insurance research effort. We wish to acknowledge the participation of several people who served as an informal advisory panel throughout the project.

Mr. Ted Davidson
Vice President
Robert F. Driver Company, Inc.

Mr. Bernard I. Farrell
Assistant Commissioner (Retired)
California Department of Insurance

Mr. John McCann
Regional Vice President
Insurance Information Institute

Dr. William Petak
Associate Professor, Systems Management
University of Southern California

Mr. David Simons
Regional Representative
Insurance Information Institute

We would also like to thank the risk managers and other administrative officers who contributed valuable information on insurance issues relevant to local government and special districts.

Mr. H.S. Bachrach
Chief, Risk Management
County of Los Angeles

Dr. Harold Boring
Assistant Superintendent for Administrative Services
San Bernardino City Schools

Mr. Hal Brewer
Risk Manager
City of Riverside

Mr. Lawrence P. Gallagher
Risk Manager
Metropolitan Water District of Southern California

Mr. Edward H. Kossart
Risk Manager
City of Los Angeles

Mr. Rich Paikoff
Administrative Assistant
City of Irvine

Mr. Olinto Ricci
Finance Director
City of Westminster

Mr. Terry Roberts
Risk Manager
County of Fresno

Ms. Pamela H. Thompson
Risk Manager
County of San Bernardino

Mr. Rod Umscheid
Risk Manager
County of Orange

We appreciate the careful review and thoughtful comments of our peer review committee.

Dr. Dan Barber
Associate Professor, Public Policy
California State University, Long Beach

Mr. Charles Ford
Commissioner
California Seismic Safety Commission

Mr. Robert Gibson
Chairman of the Board
Valley Federal Savings and Loan

Mr. Thomas Hamner
Assistant Director, Disaster Assistance Program
Federal Emergency Management Agency, Region IX

Mr. Edward Kossart
Risk Manager
City of Los Angeles

Mr. John McCann
Regional Vice President
Insurance Information Institute

Dr. Linda B. Nilson
Assistant Professor, Sociology
University of California, Los Angeles

Mr. Dale Peterson
Administrator, National Flood Insurance Program
Federal Emergency Management Agency, Region IX

Mr. Evar Peterson
City Councilman
City of Westminster

Mr. David Simmons
Regional Representative
Insurance Information Institute

We wish to acknowledge the contribution of research materials from two sources.

Dr. E.L. Quarantelli
Director, Disaster Research Center
The Ohio State University

Dr. Risa Palm
Associate Director, Natural Hazards Research and Applications Information Center
University of Colorado, Boulder

Table of Contents

Preface

This report grew out of the City of Los Angeles Planning Partnership for which the Southern California Earthquake Preparedness Project (SCEPP) was asked to research and report on several issues pertaining to earthquake insurance. In the course of this research, it became obvious to both SCEPP and SCEPP's Policy Advisory Board that earthquake insurance and its role in the recovery process was a major policy issue. Thus, the research effort was expanded to incorporate broader issues and circulation of the report beyond the Los Angeles Planning Partnership.

The report has five goals which correspond to its organization: (1) to outline the provisions (coverages, rates, deductibles, etc.) of earthquake insurance policies currently available to the major classes of insurance consumers—homeowners, businesses, local governments and special districts; (2) to determine the extent to which earthquake insurance is purchased by these parties and explore the circumstances surrounding purchase or non-purchase; (3) to review the salient issues in earthquake insurance from the standpoints of purchasers and providers; (4) to explore potential Federal roles in resolving these issues and in providing or promoting earthquake insurance; and finally, (5) to make reasonable policy recommendations involving both the Federal Government and other stakeholders in earthquake insurance toward a more adequate system of coverage.

Executive Summary

One will quickly note from the title of this report that we consider the circumstances surrounding the provision and purchase of earthquake insurance problematic. Historically, the insurance industry has compiled a reasonably good record of meeting its contractual obligations in major American disasters, including several major earthquakes. So why should earthquake insurance be regarded a problem? The answer lies in the destructive potential of infrequent "great" earthquakes. Should an event measuring 8.0 or more on the Richter scale occur along a major fault affecting heavily populated urban centers, the losses would be staggering. The danger, according to insurance representatives and industry analysts, is the questionable capacity to meet the payout demands in such an event and consequent insolvencies by individual companies. As a result of these concerns and others, the insurance industry has not vigorously marketed earthquake insurance nor made it a particularly attractive buy to most potential purchasers. Demand has been predictably sluggish.

Efforts to expand availability and stimulate demand face several formidable obstacles in addition to the basic concern with payout capacity and insolvency. One barrier is "adverse selection" or the inability to spread the earthquake risk across an appropriately large number of exposed properties. Securing an adequate level of reinsurance is a related issue. Another obstacle is the unavailability of accurate and reliable data upon which to calculate rates. Since great earthquakes are rare and demographic changes as well as property development are continuous, calculation of probable losses and determination of rates are difficult. Large payouts for earthquake damage would require insurance companies to tap accumulated reserves. But constraints on the buildup of catastrophe reserves imposed by the Internal Revenue Service (IRS) exacerbates the capacity problem and acts as a disincentive to more widespread and aggressive participation of insurance companies in the earthquake insurance market. Another major concern is the ineffectiveness of loss reducing activities by state and local governments particularly in building code enforcement and land-use planning. As a result of these problems, individual insurance companies have been unwilling to write earthquake policies beyond certain self-imposed limits. The policies which are made available typically have high deductibles and premiums.

Consumer interest in earthquake insurance has not been high. While earthquake premiums taken in by insurance companies continue to rise (See Appendix A) the percentage of homeowners and small businesses covered remains stable at approximately 5 percent. Large corporations have shown much greater interest in earthquake coverage. A recent survey indicated that over half the firms which responded held some type of earthquake insurance policy (Hudson and Petak, 1981). Much less is known about local government and special district purchasers. Based upon limited data, small jurisdictions tend to remain uninsured while large governmental units often self insure.

The barriers to enhanced purchaser interest in earthquake insurance go beyond limited availability and the reluctance to market earthquake insurance by the primary providers. Consumers do often cite high premiums and deductibles as reasons for not purchasing earthquake coverage. But extensive research on individual decision-making indicates that people are reluctant to take action to protect themselves against any events which could be hazardous to themselves or their property but have a low probability of occurrence. Further, there is considerable misinformation regarding earthquake insurance. People mistakenly believe that earthquakes are automatically covered as part of their homeowners policies or that earthquake coverage is not available at all. Many homeowners view insurance as an investment rather than a protective mechanism. This view leads to rejection of earthquake insurance as a poor investment, particularly when combined with the assumption that Federal disaster relief and low interest loans will be readily available after a major earthquake event.

In the course of our research, we discovered two trends which are likely to have an impact on purchaser interest in earthquake insurance. One is the current "soft" market in all lines of insurance. Declining insurance industry profits have led to better rates and lower premiums for some classes of consumers, particularly large purchasers (i.e. local governments and large firms). A second trend which will stimulate demand for earthquake coverage is the proliferation of risk management expertise among governmental jurisdictions and large business establishments. Risk managers are highly aware of environmental hazards and sophisticated insurance purchasers. Homeowners and small businesses, by far the largest groups at risk, will remain largely unaffected by these trends.

The obstacles to adequate provision and purchase of earthquake insurance contribute to a basic policy problem: excessive risk taking by those with the greatest exposure to earthquake hazards. The importance of earthquake insurance should not be exaggerated; even with a greatly expanded system of insurance, this mechanism would be only one source of recovery resources. It could, in our view, play a much larger role in recovery than it does under present circumstances. The benefits of overcoming the problem through stimulation of both provision and purchase of earthquake insurance would be in the greater spread of risk, a more equitable distribution of responsibility for recovery, and possibly, a more rapid return to normal life within the impacted region.

A solution to the earthquake insurance dilemma will require the participation of all stakeholders: the various classes of purchasers, insurance companies, reinsurers, the financial community and all levels of government. Our contribution to resolution of the earthquake insurance dilemma will, for the most part, be limited to an exploration of Federal Government strategies to provide or promote earthquake insurance. We argue that the Federal Government can, and must, play a lead role in this endeavor. This role is justified by the national scope of the earthquake problem, the repercussions of a devastating earthquake on the nation's economy and by the inability of other stakeholders to resolve the dilemma without the resources of the Federal Government.

After a review of the three broad strategies, we concluded that the most feasible and effective alternative approach by the Federal Government would be to adopt policies which assist the insurance industry in extending coverage under essentially free market conditions. The actions recommended include market intervention by the Federal Government to promote greater insurance availability but not as principal provider of earthquake insurance. Our recommendations are divided into measures affecting provision of earthquake insurance and those relating to purchase.

Recommendations: Provisions

1. **We recommend creation of a Federal Insurance Corporation to sell excess catastrophe reinsurance to the primary insurance and reinsurance industries.** This Federal agency would not compete with private reinsurers but would provide a layer of reinsurance over and above that which can be acquired in the private sector. This measure, we believe, would serve to expand the availability of coverage, help mitigate the problems of risk spreading and expand the insurance industry's capacity to meet the payout requirements of Probable Maximum Loss (PML) events.

2. **We believe that these same ends could be served by the creation of a standby Federal Catastrophe Loan Plan.** This plan would make loans available to insurance companies if, due to a major disaster, their reserves were depleted beyond some predetermined threshold level.

3. **Since the availability of large catastrophe reserves is critical in meeting the expected payout demands for an unprecedented earthquake disaster, we recommend modification of IRS restrictions on the build up of insurance company reserves.**

4. **We recommend continued support and funding for the California Earthquake Zoning and Probable Maximum Loss Evaluation Program being conducted by the California Department of Insurance.** This effort has resulted in the collection of data on earthquake losses which should provide a more accurate data base for disaster planners and insurance actuaries.

5. **We recommend that insurance companies offer incentives in the form of rebates or premium reductions for individuals, firms or local jurisdictions which provide evidence of hazard mitigation efforts, preparedness and land-use measures.** These incentives should be backed up by Federal loans and grants-in-aid for loss reduction efforts.

Recommendations: Purchasers

1. **Assuming that measures are undertaken to deal with the problems of provision, we recommend that lending institutions at the initiative of the Federal Government and through the Federal Home Loan Mortgage Association, and/or the Federal National Mortgage Association require the purchase of earthquake insurance in hazard-prone areas as a condition for granting new home loans.**

2. **Small government jurisdictions should form pooling arrangements to take advantage of better insurance rates usually reserved for large purchasers. We also recommend that small jurisdictions purchase tax interruption coverage to assure a continued flow of revenue in the event that primary tax sources are lost.**

3. **We regard self-insurance as a viable alternative to commercially acquired coverage for large local governments whose premiums would be enormous even with good rates. However, we recommend that self-insurance be incorporated into a sound program of risk management.** Such a program would include: a thorough knowledge of what facilities are at greatest risk; a program of risk reduction which includes land-use planning, preparedness and earthquake hazard mitigation; a plan which identifies revenue sources, program funds and reserves to be diverted for emergency response and recovery; a detailed understanding of Federal disaster assistance programs available to local governments; the purchase of privately provided insurance for a level of risk beyond which a local entity cannot reasonably expect to assume responsibility; and catastrophe reserves, at least sufficient to carry a jurisdiction through the emergency period.

4. **We recommend that corporations and nonself-insured government jurisdictions which have not purchased earthquake insurance take advantage of current soft market conditions in the insurance industry and acquire coverage.** Particularly favorable rates and deductibles are available to those purchasers whose premiums place them in the $100,000 and up classification.

While these recommendations would substantially address the current earthquake insurance dilemma, we also believe that insurance stakeholders should seriously consider the ultimate goal of an all-hazards insurance program. Such a program would require a genuine public-private partnership and the continued participation of all representative parties. The precise role of the Federal Government cannot be foreseen. We have endorsed a Federal strategy of market stimulation and promotion of earthquake insurance. This strategy, based upon research and interviews with representative stakeholders, appears to offer a balance of acceptability, feasibility and effectiveness. It is nevertheless an approach which is critically dependent upon the voluntary cooperation of all involved interests. Without this cooperation market failure will most likely remain a problem. While a federally mandated program of earthquake or all-catastrophe insurance may be unfavorably received by some stakeholders, it represents the most effective strategy to ensure participation and adequate risk spreading while avoiding a potential disaster induced national economic crisis.

I. Earthquake Insurance: An Introductory Overview

A. Earthquakes and Earthquake Threat

Earthquakes are potentially the most destructive of all natural disasters in both loss of life and property damage. Casualties and structural damage result from intense ground shaking and such secondary effects as fires, landslides, ground subsidence, and flooding from dam collapse or tsunamis. While earthquakes in the United States are commonly associated with the West Coast, particularly California, 39 states altogether face some degree of seismic risk. Seventy million people and at least nine metropolitan areas are susceptible to severe earthquakes. Nevertheless, California has been the focal point of most earthquake studies due to its high frequency of events (two thirds of all earthquakes have occurred in California), large population and extensive property development. But the high frequency of earthquakes alone does not warrant the amount of official and scientific attention these events have received. It is the rare and devastating earthquake such as the 1906 San Francisco quake and the 1964 Alaska event, both of which measured more than 8 on the Richter Scale. Earthquakes of this magnitude could be expected in the United States, and most likely in California, every 60 to 100 years and less severe but major earthquakes every 15 to 20 years (Anderson, et al., 1981). The area currently believed to be at greatest risk of a massive earthquake is the Los Angeles-San Bernardino region. An event which could exceed 8 on the Richter Scale has an estimated annual probability of occurrence of 2 to 5 percent and its likelihood of occurrence in the next 20 to 30 years is regarded as "high". This earthquake could kill and injure between 15,000 and 69,000 persons (depending upon time of occurrence) and cause up to $17 billion in property damage (NSC/FEMA, 1980). Some studies have placed the property damage estimates as high as $50 billion (U.S. Department of Commerce, 1969).

B. Earthquake Related Property Damage

The wide discrepancy in damage estimates cited in the previous section underscores a basic problem in risk assessment: the unavailability of adequate and comprehensive statistics on earthquake related property damage. The lack of earthquake damage statistics is due mainly to the extremely low frequency with which major earthquakes strike heavily populated areas and the lack of adequate resources and incentives to generate such studies.

Earthquakes cause damage through ground vibration or shaking, the geologically associated hazards of faulting, landsliding and ground failure and earthquake generated "secondary" disasters like fires, dam failures, avalanches and tsunamis. Losses due to earthquake damage may be direct (e.g. damage to buildings, contents, machinery, equipment), or indirect (e.g. business interruption losses, loss of property value, loss of jobs, Worker's Compensation losses, loss of rental income, additional living expenses, potential liability losses, and mortgage default losses). It is estimated that the majority of direct losses would be to commercial, industrial and government owned property and facilities, especially damage and disruption to utilities, transportation systems and communication systems (Anderson, et al., 1981). Residential losses could approach 50 percent of all building losses. There is, however, one major difference between residential and commercial damage potential: most of the residential losses occur in the small damage

1

percentage range while commercial losses occur mainly in high percentage range. After the San Fernando Valley earthquake of 1971, it was determined that commercial and industrial property losses in the City of Los Angeles amounted to $61.6 million while losses to single family dwellings were estimated at $42 million. Damages to apartments were set at $36.7 million. Sixty-two percent of the dollar loss to commercial and industrial property fell into the high damage category (losses due to structures sustaining such extensive damage that they were designated unsafe for human occupancy). Only 25 percent of the dollar loss to single family dwellings was attributed to such severe damage (Los Angeles Department of Building and Safety, 1971). While loss figures for residential property may be quite large when aggregated, the percentage loss on a per dwelling basis is usually quite small. In the Long Beach earthquake of 1933, the second worst earthquake on record to hit Southern California, 95 percent of the residential structures sustained less than 5 percent loss to the dwelling's total replacement value (U.S. Department of Commerce, 1969). The estimated loss to the public sector after the 1971 San Fernando Valley earthquake was $238.5 million. This figure represents nearly 48 percent of the estimated total loss area-wide as result of that event. The jurisdiction which experienced the greatest losses was the City of Los Angeles ($100 million) (Algermissen, et al., 1977). Comprehensive estimates of indirect losses, those resulting from business disruption, loss of income, and liability have not been compiled.

C.   Earthquake Insurance: How It Developed and How It Works

Historically, the development of disaster insurance systems has followed large scale catastrophes. Earthquake insurance in the United States probably received its impetus from the great San Francisco earthquake of 1906. Beginning in 1916, earthquake insurance became available as an independent policy (Steinbrugge, 1982). Insurance companies later offered earthquake coverage as both a separate policy and as an endorsement to property fire policies. American insurance companies differ from their counterparts in other nations which offer earthquake insurance as part of a comprehensive package policy. This practice can be traced to the development of American insurance companies last century which formed to provide one type of insurance only (e.g. fire, casualty, life, etc.). Subsequent insurance practices and state regulation served to rigidify the writing of insurance on a "name-peril" rather than an "all-risk" or "excluded peril" basis.

Despite its attractive rate (4 cents per $100 with a 5 percent deductible) in 1916, few policies were written. The low demand was probably caused by a misperception regarding earthquake damage. Since over 80 percent of the losses from the 1906 San Francisco event were caused by fire, people assumed that most damage in any earthquake would be caused by fire. Thus, they may have concluded that earthquake insurance was unnecessary since a bulk of their earthquake losses would be covered by fire insurance. The insurance industry apparently shared this view which resulted in low rates, small company reserves and minimal reinsurance (Kunreuther, 1978).

The Santa Barbara earthquake of 1925 was significant in that it caught a great majority of those affected, uninsured ($8 million in current damage dollars). Further, there was no major fire following the earthquake, so fire insurance played no role in recovery. It also became known that damaging earthquakes could be expected in the future in the

Southern California region. The emerging public perception of earthquake threat and greater knowledge of the type of damage earthquakes cause led to a significant increase in earthquake insurance sales immediately following the Santa Barbara event (See Appendix A). As memory of the earthquake faded, however, insurance purchases dropped off markedly. There was no major surge in earthquake insurance purchases after the 1933 Long Beach tremor but purchases rose steadily during the decade from 1940-50 despite the absence of any major damaging event. This increase may have been due to rising property values and purchases by commercial firms. The 1971 San Fernando Valley earthquake stimulated the most dramatic increase in earthquake insurance purchases in the program's history. These purchases were made mainly by commercial firms, however, and as of 1982, only 5 percent of all homeowners in California were covered by earthquake insurance.

1.   Homeowners

For homeowners, earthquake insurance is typically written as an endorsement to the standard comprehensive homeowners policy and is subject to a minimum deductible of 5, 10 or 15 percent, depending on the type of construction. Small wood frame structures are regarded as Class I risks and usually require a 5 percent deductible. A deductible of 10 percent applies to structures with walls of reinforced concrete, brick or concrete block with floors and/or roof other than reinforced concrete (Class VII). Insurance policies written for structures with walls of unreinforced adobe or hollow concrete block require a 15 percent deductible. A great majority of single family dwellings in the Western United States are Class I risks and qualify for a deductible of 5 percent. Thus, a house valued at $100,000 would carry a deductible of $5,000. The 5 percent deductible, however, is not a rigid guideline. In the past year some independent agents and brokers have offered earthquake coverage with a $1,000 deductible and a $100,000 limit of coverage. Earthquake insurance is available from licensed property insurance and casualty insurance agents. Most of the insurance firms which write earthquake policies use rates developed by the Insurance Services Office (ISO). These rates are advisory for companies and competition may produce deviation from rates established by the ISO. ISO rates are a function of the risk zone in which a structure is located and its type of construction. Each state has its own set of rates. While in some states the rates are uniform for the entire state, states which have a higher earthquake risk may be divided into two or three zones. For low risk states, rates vary from 2 to 6 cents per $100 of insurance purchased. For a $100,000 insurance policy, this represents a $20 to $60 premium per year. For higher risk states, the rates range between 16 and 20 cents per $100 of insurance or a premium of $160 to $200 per year. Insured individuals are reimbursed at full replacement cost less the deductible.

2.   Commercial Firms

Commercial firms, like individual homeowners, typically purchase earthquake insurance as an endorsement to existing polices rather than buying separate policies. There are alternative purchase options to the Earthquake Extension Endorsement, however, and these include Difference in Conditions (DIC) policies, Manufacturer's Output Policies (MOPs), Builder's Risk (BR) policies and various Inland Marine policies. DIC policies are the principal means of insuring against earthquake risks by large commercial firms. DIC policies are usually purchased to supplement a business' basic property coverages (fire and extended) which typically exclude certain perils. DIC insurance covers earthquake, flood, water damage, landslides, mudslides, collapse and theft. The main property covered includes buildings, equipment, machinery and sometimes property in transit. Limits of liability vary widely from policy to policy depending upon the needs of the insured and what the insurer is willing to extend in terms of coverage. Deductibles are mandatory under DIC insurance and are often expressed as a percentage of the property exposure. These deductibles closely parallel those required of homeowners and in standard business property insurance endorsements. Since DIC is meant to be catastrophic protection, deductibles are often quite high. Premium rates are determined separately for each risk. DIC policies are popular among commercial firms because of their flexibility in selecting insurance amounts in the perils covered and in determining the limits of liability and premium rates.

Earthquake coverage on manufactured goods is often obtained through the MOP. The main intent of this coverage is to protect property in transit. Earthquake coverage can be added for goods at permanent locations for an additional premium.

BR insurance is written to cover damages to property in the course of construction. This type of policy offers protection against earthquake damage to construction projects. Such projects are regarded as high risk due to lack of building stability while under construction, the possibility that loss prevention systems like sprinklers and fire resistant materials may not have been installed and the question of who owns or assumes responsibility for the building or structure while under construction. Despite the risk, coverage is normally provided by insurers due to the temporary nature of the policy. When the project has been completed BR insurance will cease.

While DIC insurance is the dominant form of inland marine coverage (insurance on property in process of transportation within a country) for earthquake losses, other inland marine policies provide similar coverage. Although these policies cover such moveable property as cameras, furs, jewels, art objects, data processing equipment, and communication equipment, other fixed location risks related to transportation have been included (e.g. tunnels, bridges, docks, wharfs, etc.).

The Earthquake Extension Endorsement through which earthquake insurance is added to existing policies, is used by most small to medium sized businesses. The Earthquake Extension Endorsement is subject to an 80 percent minimum coinsurance requirement. If the amount of insurance purchased is less than 80 percent of the value of the property, the policy-holder will collect less than total value of the property minus the deductible. The deductible is a percentage of the actual cash value of the insured property, 2 percent in most states, 5 percent in high risk states, 10 to 15 percent for types of construction particularly vulnerable to earthquakes. The deductibles apply separately to each building or structure and the property in each yard. Rates take into account location, construction type and nature of the contents. The ISO provides one set of rates for the 13 high risk Western states and another for the remainder of the country. Within each state, counties are assigned to one of the five zones based upon the frequency and intensity of earthquake occurrences. Construction type is divided into 11 grades with 1 representing the lowest risk type (wood frame dwellings) and 11, the highest risk type (adobe or hollow tile walled buildings). For each of the 5 earthquake zones and the 11 building grades, there are separate rates for contents. Fragile contents are rated higher than durable goods. So, given the state, zone, building rate grade, and contents rate grade, a specific rate can be assigned to a specific risk. These rates vary from a low of 2 cents per $100 to a high of $1.50 per $100. Other than zone, building type and contents, underwriters may consider soil composition, local building codes, the degree of automation and other factors in setting rates.

Three other types of commercial earthquake insurance coverage include Earthquake Sprinkler Leakage (ESL), Consequential Loss coverage and Mortgage Insurance for Default Losses. Earthquake induced discharges of sprinkler systems can cause considerable damage to building contents. To cover this contingency a firm may purchase the Sprinkler Leakage Earthquake Extension Endorsement. Rates are based on zone, building classification and the susceptibility of contents to water damage. This endorsement is redundant if earthquake insurance (by endorsement or separate policy) has been purchased. Consequential Loss coverages include Business Interruption, Extra Expense, Additional Living Expenses, Rent or Rental Value and Leasehold Interest. These policies were designed to address the problems of indirect losses which can, in some cases, exceed the direct initial losses. Since damages are likely to be greater in multi-story buildings, these policies assess a surcharge for buildings over eight stories. There is also a 168 hour waiting period deductible for taller buildings, that is, liability for interruption of business or untenantability exists only after the first 168 hours. Although fire and extended coverage policies are, almost without exception, required for securing a mortgage loan, no such requirement exists for earthquake protection. Thus, savings and loan associations face the risk that mortgagors whose property is damaged in an earthquake will default. If the damaged property's value is less than the outstanding mortgage balance the loss will be incurred by the mortgage lender. Some lenders have purchased earthquake insurance to protect themselves against default loss. Others erroneously assume that mortgage guarantee insurance will cover this contingency.

Thus far, the types of coverages available to commercial firms have been outlined. The actual patterns of commercial coverage are revealed in a survey of Risk and Insurance Management Society (RIMS) members conducted by the J. H. Wiggins Company in 1980 (Hudson and Petak, 1981). The survey, which netted 162 returns (32.4 percent response rate) indicated that 56 percent of the sample had some form of earthquake insurance totaling $6.27 billion. This represents $68.9 million per insured respondent. The great majority (88 percent) valued their property on a replacement cost basis; 7.7 percent insured on the basis of actual cash value of the property; 2.2 percent used some other form of valuation and the remaining 2.2 percent did not answer the question. The insurance coverage purchased on the average is greatest for utilities and storage facilities ($80.9 million) followed closely by high-rise buildings ($80 million) then manufacturing facilities ($52.7 million). Insurance coverage took the following forms: DIC, $3.2 billion (51.1 percent); Earthquake Extension Endorsement, $1.26 billion (20 percent); ESL, $590 million (9.4 percent); and others, including Manuscript policies, MOP, etc., $1.22 billion (19.45 percent). The authors noted that substantial amounts of earthquake insurance are purchased by large corporations outside of California (mean coverage in millions of dollars was 41.7 for

California, 76.3 for all U.S. facilities). Finally, they estimated that the commercial sector accounts for as much as $700 billion of earthquake insurance throughout the U.S.

3. Local Government

While the types of earthquake insurance available to homeowners and businesses as well as the purchase patterns by these two groups are reasonably well documented, very little aggregated information is available on coverages and purchase patterns of local governments and special jurisdictions. A comprehensive analysis of purchase patterns is beyond the scope of this report, however, an attempt will be made to identify the types of earthquake insurance policies available to local governments, the decisions which resulted in purchase or non-purchase, and the details of the coverages in force. A small non-probability sample of city, county and special jurisdiction (school and water) risk managers was selected. This sample included four city, four county and two special district risk management officials. Interviews were conducted between April 12 and May 20, 1983 using an instrument (See Appendix B) with open-ended questions; elaborated responses were encouraged.

The types of earthquake insurance coverage available to local governmental units closely approximate those available to commercial firms. Earthquake insurance may be secured as an endorsement to a standard or "all-risk" property (real and personal) and rental income policy or as a separate earthquake policy. Earthquake coverage for demolition, increased cost of construction, course of construction and tax interruption can also be purchased. Demolition includes the cost of razing any undamaged portion of a structure and clearing the site. Increased cost of construction or repair is available for earthquake damage. These policies cover expenses to repair or rebuild a municipal facility consistent with current building codes. Course of construction coverage insures against all risks of direct physical loss or damage to insured property while at the contract site or while in transit to the site. Finally, earthquake coverage can be obtained by local jurisdictions which guarantees a continued flow of revenue of specified type (e.g. sales, property, etc.) when direct physical damage wholly or partially prevents the generation of revenue.

In the policies examined, loss by earthquake was defined as all loss caused by earthquake shocks arising from a single seismic event and occurring within a period of 72 hours from the first such shock to cause loss (Robert F. Driver and Co., 1983). The earthquake coverage which is included in property and rental income policies usually contains a 5 percent deductible but may have a deductible as low as 2 percent with a maximum of $100,000 per city per occurrence. The deductible applies to the cash value of the unit or units insured or the full annual rental income value. The unit of insurance may be a separate facility or a complex, the contents of each separate building or structure and the property in each yard. The rate for those governmental units which had property coverage including earthquake ranged between 5.2 and 7 cents per $100 of coverage and facilities were covered for replacement cost. Some policies contain upper limits of aggregate liability. For example, the policies held by two local governments whose risk managers were interviewed, had $20 million limits on insurance company liability for earthquake losses. Tax interruption coverage, held by two local governments in the sample, had a 2.5 percent deductible (of the annual

6

tax value) with no upper limit on coverage. None of the risk managers indicated that their current policies included course of construction coverage. Total coverage held by the nine jurisdictions which had policies in force (including those which had earthquake insurance on bond indentures only) ranged from $12.7 to $90 million.

Local governments and special jurisdictions do not always rely on private insurance providers for coverage. Some cities, counties and special districts self-insure. That is, a legislative or administrative decision is made to retain the responsibility for losses to government property caused by various perils including earthquake. The option to self-insure appears to be one taken mainly by large governmental units (e.g. large cities and counties). The elements of a self insurance program include: a thorough knowledge of the extent of retained risk, a program of risk reduction including preparedness and hazard mitigation, identification of disaster assistance programs available for recovery, and catastrophe reserves. Some risk managers have combined programs of self-insurance with privately acquired coverages. These programs typically include coverage obtained from insurance providers for most property and a self-insured retention for the deductible portion or whatever losses the governmental unit can reasonably absorb.

Although the small number of cases in the study of earthquake insurance purchases by local government does not permit confident generalization, some trends were apparent. The larger the government in terms of annual budget and net assets, the more likely it was to self-insure, particularly for earthquake damage. Risk managers for large governmental units cited several factors in the decision to self-insure. The high cost of earthquake premiums to insure hundreds of millions of dollars in property was prohibitive given the risk. They also felt that a large local government representing hundreds of thousands of constituents would have sufficient political influence and legal expertise to secure an optimum amount of Federal disaster relief funds in the event of an earthquake disaster. With large annual budgets and a geographically dispersed exposure base, large local governments tended to regard the probability as slight that facilities could be damaged beyond their ability to pay for losses. For local governments of all types and sizes, earthquake insurance purchases were not always a matter of choice. Local governments were insured for earthquake losses based upon their degree of bonded indebtedness. Some types of revenue bonds require insurance coverage, including earthquake damage endorsements, as part of the covenant to secure the bonds. Four risk managers interviewed indicated that their facilities were earthquake insured because bond obligations required it. All four had purchased coverage through insurance brokers rather than self-insure because the bond council or trustee had discouraged or prohibited risk retention.

Two small cities and one county whose risk managers were interviewed indicated that they had purchased earthquake insurance for the first time during the past fiscal year. The reason cited was that earthquake coverage had become a more attractive buy. A "soft" market for insurance currently exists in that providers, anxious to obtain premiums for high yield investments, are offering coverage at bargain prices. One risk manager said that earthquake insurance had been added to the property policy free with renewal of the existing coverage package. Another reported that the quote for earthquake coverage represented a 35 percent reduction over the previous year's price. Reduction in the deductible has also made earthquake insurance coverage more attractive to local jurisdictions. Thus because of market conditions there may be a trend toward expanded coverage in both the public and private sectors. Finally, two small cities were members of an intergovernmental arrangement through which they received better insurance rates.

II. Issues and Problems with the Present System of Earthquake Insurance

Considering the amount of property at risk and the ever-present threat of a catastrophic earthquake, it seems indeed an anomaly that only 5 percent of all California homeowners and just over half of all large corporations in the nation have purchased earthquake insurance. Why have so few individuals and corporations taken advantage of available avenues of protection from the hazards associated with large magnitude earthquakes? Perhaps the most succinct statement of the overall problem involving both insurance providers and insurance purchasers is the following: insurance providers are reluctant to aggressively market earthquake insurance and potential purchasers are unaware of, misinformed about, or simply choose not to purchase it.

A. A View of Earthquake Insurance from the Standpoint of Potential Purchasers

1. Homeowners

Homeowners, according to Kunreuther (1978), do not generally worry about events like earthquakes and other natural disasters which may cause severe losses to their property but have a low probability of occurrence. The low probability and general lack of experience with large earthquake events contribute to a lack of concern with the consequences of such events. Thus, most individuals do not engage in a detailed analysis of the costs and benefits of purchasing earthquake insurance. Based on laboratory experiments, Kunreuther (ibid) discovered that the importance placed on the probability of catastrophic events among individuals rather than on the loss likely to occur had another consequence. Homeowners tended to regard insurance as an investment rather than a protective mechanism. From this standpoint, people do not purchase earthquake insurance because they consider it unlikely that they will realize any return on their investment. That is, the chance that a loss would exceed the deductible has a low probability. Past experience with damaging earthquakes and knowing someone who had purchased earthquake insurance were the best indicators that individuals would have purchased such coverage.

Overall, the situation of the uninsured homeowner is one in which both earthquake risk and earthquake insurance have low salience. While most homeowners were aware that earthquake coverage existed, over 60 percent did not know that they were eligible to purchase this coverage. A vast majority were unaware of such basic earthquake policy particulars as premiums and deductibles. This indifference toward earthquake insurance cannot be accounted for in terms of the assumption that government will provide blanket assistance to those suffering losses. The majority of those surveyed by Kunreuther anticipated no aid at all from the government in the event of a disaster. In short, most homeowners in hazard prone areas have not considered to any degree how they would recover from losses suffered by a major earthquake event. Kunreuther concludes that, "the consumer is the source of market failure (and) it may be necessary to substitute other institutional mechanisms for the free market if individuals are to be protected against the consequences of low probability high loss events" (1979:244).

9

2.   Commercial Firms

Earthquake insurance purchases by commercial firms and the decision processes which result in those purchases have not been as systematically or thoroughly analyzed as have homeowner patterns. The survey conducted by Hudson and Petak (1981) provides an outline of earthquake coverage obtained by corporations but does not provide information on the factors considered in purchase decisions. The authors of that study, based on 162 returns from RIMS members learned that approximately 56 percent of the national sample surveyed had some form of earthquake insurance. This, of course, represents a substantially greater propensity to purchase earthquake insurance coverage by commercial establishments than by individual homeowners. A number of caveats should be considered, however, in drawing conclusions based on this relatively high figure. The authors acknowledge a possible bias toward a higher coverage figure in that RIMS firms are likely to employ professional risk managers who are more concerned about the consequences associated with environmental hazards than non-member firms. Not only are they likely to be more aware of the potential for catastrophic losses but they are likely to be employed by large corporations as well. The authors discovered that the median value of earthquake insurance bought by a typical respondent was $20.9 million for properties located throughout the U.S. The total figure for all 162 firms was $6.27 billion in earthquake insurance coverage. Clearly, Hudson and Petak have tapped a sample of large well capitalized firms with professional risk managers whose function it is to provide financial security for their firms against accidental and unplanned losses. If some form of earthquake insurance is the norm for large firms, commercial organizations which are small to mid-sized and do not have a specialized risk management functionary are probably much less likely to have purchased earthquake insurance.

Nevertheless, commercial firms are more likely to hold earthquake insurance policies than individual homeowners. Kunreuther (1980) suggests that this difference in purchase patterns between businesses and homeowners may be accounted for in terms of the different ways each group defines the problem. Homeowners tend to focus on the low probability of a catastrophic earthquake while risk managers are most concerned about potential losses. Business people thus see insurance as an attractive buy relative to the heavy losses they may suffer after the earthquake, should their organization remain uninsured. Given the greater demand for earthquake insurance among commercial firms and the greater degree of sophistication regarding environmental hazards, insurance firms may adopt more aggressive promotional and marketing strategies for businesses than they do for individual homeowners.

3.   Local Governments

As indicated previously, little research has been conducted on earthquake insurance purchase decisions by local governments or how natural disaster coverage fits into an overall program of risk management. One recent survey (Wright and Rossi, 1981), however, indicated that reducing the risks of environmental hazards is low on the list of priorities of local and state officials. State and local government decision-makers, when asked to prioritize a list of 18 problems faced by public officials, listed inflation, welfare, unemployment and crime as the most pressing ones and fires, floods, hurricanes and earthquakes as the least pressing. The California

10

results did not differ from those obtained in other parts of the country. Nevertheless, in our efforts to locate risk management officials for interviews regarding earthquake insurance, we had little difficulty in securing a small sample of Southern California jurisdictions with some type of earthquake insurance program in force. Based on this research a number of issues and problems became evident.

Self-insurance for losses due to earthquake damage may involve taking on more risk than a local jurisdiction can effectively handle. A recurrence in Southern California of the great earthquake of 1857 would create losses on a regional scale. Even large jurisdictions with facilities spread over an entire metropolitan or urban-rural area could suffer losses which seriously strain their financial capacity to recover without substantial extra-local assistance. Of the 11 risk managers interviewed, five reported a self-insured retention which was equal to or in excess of 75 percent of their total property exposure. All risk officials whose jurisdictions are self-insured for earthquake losses indicated that repair and recovery funds would come from current budgets and disaster assistance. However, none had a detailed plan for diverting monies from specific departments or programs to meet the financial burden imposed by a catastrophic earthquake. While self-insurance usually implies the accumulation of emergency reserves, only one of the five self-insured jurisdictions had such a fund (which was equal to 1 percent of the annual budget).

In all self-insured jurisdictions there was an expectation that Federal disaster assistance would play an important role in recovery. There was, however, a limited understanding as to what assistance programs were applicable to local governments, the amount of aid likely to be forthcoming or the eligibility requirements to obtain Federal assistance.

A second issue in earthquake insurance purchase patterns among local governments is the availability of coverage from private insurance providers. At present there is no particular reluctance on the part of the insurance industry to make earthquake insurance coverage available to local governments. Insurance companies, according to the Insurance Information Institute, are more concerned with type of building construction and facility use than preferences for sale to homeowners, businesses or local governments. Current "soft" market conditions in the insurance industry have made most lines of insurance available to all classes of consumers at extremely attractive rates. Large insurance consumers, i.e. business firms and local governments, are especially likely to benefit from this buyer's market. Earthquake insurance is offered at extremely low rates or even included at no additional charge when comprehensive package policies are purchased. This overall trend was detected in the purchase decisions of local government risk managers. The three jurisdictions which had purchased policies in the past fiscal year cited low premiums and in one case free insurance as reasons for obtaining earthquake policies.

From the standpoint of risk management and earthquake preparedness the enhanced availability of earthquake insurance at an attractive price is a healthy trend. At least two caveats, however, seem warranted. First, low premiums and free policies are not substitutes for a thorough understanding of earthquake risk and a commitment to reducing those risks. Those risk managers who had recently purchased earthquake insurance did so largely because it was regarded as a good buy. While these officials were all aware that Southern California could be struck, possibly without warning, by a massive earthquake, the affordability of the earthquake premiums appeared to have been the critical factor. The crucial question is whether a jurisdiction will maintain its earthquake coverage when market conditions change and insurance premiums rise. The second factor which might dampen this trend toward greater earthquake insurance availability also relates to the market but involves the providers rather than the purchasers. If the insurance industry continues to experience a decline in profit and cannot offset underwriting losses with investment income, they would probably cease marketing insurance lines in which major losses were anticipated. Earthquake insurance would most likely be one of those dropped.

A third issue which mainly affects the purchase decisions of large jurisdictions centers on whether earthquake insurance is the most cost effective means of risk reduction. Insurance is merely the transfer of risk from one party to another. Other risk reduction strategies are hazard mitigation and preparedness. Given the budgetary strains experienced by many large jurisdictions and the high premiums (despite the soft market) to insure billions of dollars in facilities, a city or county government might be better advised to invest in earthquake mitigation and preparedness rather than insurance.

It is clearly not feasible to make a generalization regarding the overall purchase patterns of local governments based on a sample of 11 cases. It is probably safe to conclude, however, that the orientations, considerations and decisionmaking regarding earthquake insurance by local governments more closely approximates those by commercial firms than those by homeowners. Large firms and many large urban governments are hiring professional risk managers who are knowledgeable about insurance programs and environmental hazards. Both commercial firms and local governments have substantial investments in facilities and equipment. Both have obligations to provide goods and services to consumers and citizens. Thus with similar property exposures, responsibilities to the public, and risk management expertise, local government earthquake insurance purchases should approximate those of commercial firms. Larger urban jurisdictions, like the large firms surveyed by Hudson and Petak (1981), should be more likely to have earthquake coverage or self-insurance programs than small rural jurisdictions.

B. A View of Earthquake Insurance from the Standpoint of Insurance Providers

Using a Nominal Group Technique (NGT) developed by Delbecq, Van de Ven and Gustafson (1975), J.H. Wiggins and Company conducted a workshop in August, 1980, on earthquake insurance issues. The workshop was attended by 31 representatives of government, industry and consumer groups and nine members of the Wiggins Company project team (these latter individuals served as discussion leaders, reporters and as sources of earthquake damage scenarios). Among the questions raised for discussion and appraisal at the workshop was the following: "what are the problems associated with the current system of insurance against earthquake losses"? Much of the information presented in this section will be based on the findings from the Earthquake Insurance Issues Workshop (Atkisson, et al., 1980) and interviews conducted with representatives of the Insurance

Information Institute, Pacific Coast Regional Office.

The perceived problems involving providers as determined by the workshop are listed below in descending order of perceived importance:

a)   actuarial and rate setting difficulties;

b)   industry capacity to meet the payout requirements resulting from Probable Maximum Loss (PML) events;

c)   Internal Revenue Service (IRS) constraints on the build-up of insurance company reserves;

d)   adverse selection and risk spreading difficulties, including those associated with reinsurance;

e)   ineffectiveness of current loss reducing activities (building code enforcement and land-use zoning);

f)   difficulties in determining both the insurability of properties and the damages resulting from earthquakes.

Other provider related problems which were mentioned but not accorded highest priority were: the possibility that the government might mandate earthquake insurance or set up a program similar to that now in effect for flood disaster, the insurance industry's lack of information on the number of policies and the dollar value of policies written by prime carriers and reinsurance entities, and the government's spending priority on prediction rather than earthquake hazard mitigation.

Actuarial and rate setting problems stem from the industry's inability to calculate the probable losses from major earthquakes. The long time periods between large damaging events militates against the development of credible statistics. In the period between earthquakes, the situation may change substantially (e.g. increased property development in high risk areas). Actuaries have been compelled to use their best judgment in setting premium rates given the lack of adequate data. A recently completed evaluation of the probable maximum earthquake loss compiled by the California Department of Insurance (California Department of Insurance, 1983) may serve to narrow this information gap. A second major concern expressed by insurance providers is that a massive earthquake occurrence in a major metropolitan area could cause individual insolvencies and seriously strain the resources of the entire insurance industry. Although earthquake premium payments have, by far, exceeded payouts since earthquake insurance first became available, industry officials are reluctant to provide such coverage beyond their own self imposed limits. This reluctance and limitation of exposure is a calculated marketing decision based on the inadequacy of technical information on earthquake loss potential, earthquake recurrence patterns and difficulties in setting differential rates for various types of structures.

A third provider problem accorded high priority by workshop participants was restraint on catastrophe reserving. Under current Federal income tax provisions, premiums which are collected by insurance companies and placed in a reserve fund for catastrophes are treated as excess profits and taxed at a rate of 50 percent (Kunreuther, 1980). Company officials regard this as a formidable impediment to aggressive marketing of earthquake insurance and have called for a longer loss carry forward period or tax-free reserves for potential earthquake losses. Also of considerable concern was the fact that the only market for earthquake insurance is in areas which are at greatest risk of large industry payouts for losses. This problem is often referred to as "adverse selection" and reflects the industry's concern that risk is not sufficiently spread over a larger geographical area including areas which are relatively unlikely to suffer a major damaging earthquake. A second risk spreading problem is that of securing adequate reinsurance for earthquake peril. Insurance companies, to limit the impact which a catastrophic earthquake might have on current revenues and reserves, purchase reinsurance through which a stipulated sum will be paid to the primary company if an earthquake event requires a payout. As with other problems involving providers, reinsurance difficulties can be traced to limited knowledge of direct and indirect losses likely to be caused by a major earthquake. Because of this limited underwriting information reinsurers must rely on their knowledge of the underwriting expertise of the primary insurer. Reinsurers also establish limits of exposure to a given type of peril and this is especially the case with catastrophe coverage. The Reinsurance Association of America estimates that approximately 9 percent of the total insurance premiums written in the United States are reinsured by both domestic and foreign reinsurers. Some industry observers believe that reinsurance companies are approaching the limits of their ability to insure primary carriers for earthquake and that any dramatic increase in the sale of earthquake coverage would result in capacity failure of both primary and reinsurance markets.

Insurance providers also expressed a lack of confidence in the commitment of state and local governments to adopt and adequately enforce building code standards and land-use zoning techniques to mitigate future earthquake losses. Finally, the lack of reliable statistics on major earthquake recurrence patterns and concomitant inability to adequately determine rates and premiums calls into question the industry's ability to determine the insurability of property.

C. Summary and Discussion of Earthquake Insurance Issues

Purchaser interest in earthquake insurance and the priority placed on earthquake risks to both public and private property is generally low. This is particularly the case with homeowners and small businesses and perhaps also the case for small governmental jurisdictions without the benefit of risk management expertise. While some observers have suggested that Federal disaster relief programs act as a disincentive to homeowner purchase of earthquake insurance, Kunreuther (1978) has argued that homeowners have a very limited knowledge of disaster assistance and that most anticipate no aid whatsoever from the Federal Government. This limited understanding of disaster aid is also characteristic of small business owners and, based on limited study, of most local government officials as well. Thus, a rational choice to take a "free ride" (Olson, 1971) at Federal expense to cover anticipated earthquake losses may be a rare occurrence in the public or private purchasing sectors.

Potential earthquake insurance purchasers also regarded coverage as difficult to buy in that it was not aggressively marketed or advertised. The available coverage was considered too costly with unfavorable limits of liability and high deductibles. Perhaps the

14

most general problems involving purchasers were lack of knowledge that earthquake coverage was available or misinformation concerning the terms of such insurance.

The Earthquake Insurance Issues Workshop (J.H. Wiggins and Company, 1980) attempted to prioritize all problems identified with earthquake insurance and determined that two provider related issues were most salient: actuarial and rate setting difficulties faced by insurance carriers and the insurance industry's capacity to meet the payout requirements for a Probable Maximum Loss (PML) event. The most serious of the purchaser related problems was the decision by homeowners and small businesses not to insure their properties for earthquake damage or lack of knowledge and misinformation which similarly result in non-purchase.

The substantial importance placed on the problems of insurance provision by Workshop participants stands in contrast to the earlier findings of Kunreuther (1978) that insurance purchasers were the major source of market failure. This earlier study concludes with a number of recommendations which if adopted would significantly increase the demand for earthquake insurance. These recommendations, while well founded, would most likely raise issues and opposition if not accompanied by proposals to deal with the provision or supply side as well. This is so because a greatly expanded demand for earthquake insurance would only serve to exacerbate the industry's problem with capacity and result in restricted availability, more unattractive provisions or both. An adequate resolution to the problems of earthquake insurance must simultaneously address both supply and demand issues.

III. Potential Federal Strategies to Address the Earthquake Insurance Dilemma

There are at least three reasons why the Federal Government rather than some other level of government should be the focal point of a solution to the earthquake insurance issue. First, as we have pointed out, earthquakes are not just a West Coast problem but can cause major damage in 39 states. So the solution which is most appropriate is one which addresses the earthquake threat in all vulnerable areas. Second, a catastrophic earthquake would cause economic dislocation of national proportions. Beyond the impact of local losses, we must be concerned with the potential insolvencies of insurance companies, banks and other financial institutions which would have severe repercussions on the nation's economy. Third, operation of the private insurance market in earthquake insurance has not produced a sufficient level of coverage to adequately provide for recovery and prevent a massive outflow of Federal money to a devastated region. Market failure is not merely an industry problem but is shared by all stakeholders; the Federal Government has restricted the industry's ability to build up catastrophe reserves; the consumer has not made serious efforts to plan for earthquake disaster by protecting property through insurance purchase; and the industry has neither promoted earthquake coverage nor been willing to write policies beyond certain self imposed limits. Thus, the scope of the problem, the widespread economic consequences, and at least partial market failure point to the Federal Government as a source of problem resolution.

A number of alternative strategies (Atkisson and Petak, 1981) are open to the Federal Government, the most general of which are: non-intervention in the earthquake insurance market, either allowing current policies to stand or redirecting Federal disaster relief programs toward more effective preparedness and hazard mitigation; intervene directly by setting up a program which would be funded and administered by the Federal Government and modeled on the present National Flood Insurance Program (NFIP); assist the insurance industry in extending coverage to a greater number of people through programs and policy modifications which do not alter free market conditions. These strategies will be examined and evaluated in this section.

A. The Strategy of Non-Intervention in the Earthquake Insurance Market

Non-intervention as a strategy is neither a meaningless residual category nor advocacy for doing nothing to alleviate the threat of huge earthquake losses. Without acting as provider or promoter of earthquake insurance, the Federal Government has acted in a variety of capacities to address the earthquake threat. It has made disaster assistance available to victims, funded research efforts to explore nearly every aspect of earthquakes and their disastrous effects and provided a variety of technical services to state and local governments. While the Federal Government has only assumed most of these functions since the end of World War II, they have become recognized as the appropriate roles for government involvement. Active intervention by the Federal Government in the private insurance market, because it taps deeply held social and economic values, is less acceptable to most stakeholders and more likely to become an issue than the government's performance of its "traditional" roles as provider of disaster assistance and research support and promoter of earthquake preparedness and hazard mitigation measures.

16

A study conducted by Atkisson, Petak and Anderson (1980) reveals considerable support among representatives of the insurance and financial industries, state and Federal Government and consumers for the traditional disaster related government functions and little enthusiasm for a direct Federal role in the earthquake insurance market (See Appendix C). Participants in the Earthquake Insurance Issues Workshop rank-ordered a long list of potential Federal roles in managing losses caused by earthquakes. Those roles which avoided direct government intervention in the insurance market included the highest ranking choice which called upon the Federal Government to "stimulate and support improved use and enforcement of earthquake loss-mitigating measures, including construction and land-use standards, by state and local governments" (p. 47). Participants recommended use of Federal aid to influence land-use controls and building construction codes.

The third-ranked Federal role saw the answer to increased purchase of earthquake insurance and implementation of loss-reducing mitigation in a revision of current disaster relief and tax policies. This was to be accomplished through a more efficient use of disaster aid to encourage, but not require, mitigation and purchase of insurance. Tax credits or deductions were recommended to stimulate earthquake insurance demand. Workshop participants ranked fourth an expanded Federal program of research, technical assistance and risk mapping in support of operations by local and state government and private industry. In sixth position was the recommendation that the Federal Government do nothing more than maintain existing policies. The Federal Government was called upon not to mandate purchase of earthquake insurance and not intrude further into the current insurance system.

Several other suggested Federal roles fell into the category of nonintervention in the earthquake insurance market. These included: prioritizing the importance of earthquake programs relative to other social needs and promoting the development of earthquake prediction and economic impact information (8th ranked), require hazard zone notifications for property transfers (9th ranked), sponsorship of public education programs on earthquake risk, mitigation, response and insurance (11th ranked) and encourage free market purchase of earthquake insurance (13th ranked).

Participants in the Workshop clearly favored maintenance or expansion of Federal involvement only in those areas where programs are now in place and private sector investment and interest is minimal. Sponsors of the Workshop concluded that there existed a clear aversion among representative stakeholders to direct Federal intrusion into the private insurance market either as regulator or provider. The strong showing made by the alternative of maintaining and not expanding current policies (6th ranked) seems to affirm this conclusion. On the whole it appears that participants favored a cautious and carefully considered expansion and/or modification of Federal disaster assistance, research and hazard mitigation policies rather than a direct intervention into the private insurance marketplace.

The impact of this strategy on the availability and expansion of earthquake insurance is difficult to estimate. Some measures like public education programs to promote the sale of earthquake insurance or Federal encouragement of land-use planning and hazard mitigation among state and local governments are unlikely to meet with much success. These actions are not likely to be taken voluntarily because of the lack of knowledge about

17

or low salience of earthquake insurance and the low priority accorded hazard abatement by most cities, counties and states. Other measures, like tax credits or deductions for purchasing earthquake insurance may mildly stimulate demand. But the strategy of Federal non-intervention in the private insurance market leaves unaddressed the serious problems which serve to restrict supply: the industry's questionable ability to meet the payout requirements for PML events and adverse selection. These factors severely limit the aggressive marketing and expanded provision of earthquake insurance. In the face of these problems, a mild increase in demand occasioned by tax credits or deductions would not have much impact. On the other hand, a strategy which avoids market involvement but does provide monetary incentives for research and hazard abatement may have substantial indirect impact on earthquake insurance provision. Federally funded research activities and technical services have generated improved loss evaluation measures, risk mapping and more earthquake resistant construction standards. These factors should promote greater accuracy in setting insurance rates and help determine the insurability of property. Greater insurability, more attractive rates and expanded coverage might also follow a tough Federal requirement that state and local governments adopt land-use planning and hazard mitigation programs in order to receive various types of Federal aid.

B.   A Program for Earthquakes Modeled on the National Flood Insurance Program

A Federal Government strategy which sought to create an earthquake or catastrophe insurance program modeled on the current flood insurance program would depart fundamentally from the strategy outlined in the last section. The basic difference is that a Federal earthquake (or all catastrophe) insurance program would involve a direct intervention into the private marketplace. Such a strategy would most likely have as its basic goals: a reduction in the size of interstate tax transfers in the form of Federal disaster assistance; that those at greatest risk bear the costs of natural hazard exposure; that disaster relief and recovery activities be joined with, and conditioned upon, appropriate hazard evaluation and mitigation practices by the beneficiaries; and prevention of unreasonable levels of risk taking by homeowners, business people and local governments. A review of the NFIP will give us some insight into how these goals have been pursued and what a program of Federal earthquake insurance might look like.

The NFIP was enacted in 1968 to provide federally subsidized flood insurance on a nationwide basis through the cooperation of the Federal Government and the private insurance industry. The Federal Government, through the Federal Insurance Administration (FIA) and the Federal Emergency Management Agency (FEMA) administer the program. These agencies identify flood-prone communities, establish insurance rates and policy terms, subsidize premiums, provide reinsurance, set standards of flood plain management and enforce hazard mitigation requirements for participating communities. Flood insurance policies are sold by licensed private insurance agents and brokers.

Prior to enactment of the NFIP, Federal response to flood disaster was the construction of flood control works (dams, levees, seawalls, etc.) and provision of disaster assistance to victims. This approach was unsatisfactory since it neither reduced losses nor discouraged unwise flood plain development. Flood insurance from private providers was not available because of adverse selection, the frequency of flooding, and the staggering

18

losses from these events. The NFIP was designed to reduce flood disaster losses through appropriate land-use management and make flood insurance available to communities at reasonable rates. Land-use management in the form of restrictions on unwise development in flood plains is accomplished by restricting the sale of federally subsidized flood insurance to those hazard prone communities that give adequate assurance that responsible land-use measures will be implemented and enforced. An identified flood-prone community (defined as that political entity which has the authority to adopt and enforce flood plain ordinances for the area under its jurisdiction) has the choice of participating in the program or forfeiting federally subsidized flood insurance and all but emergency forms of disaster assistance. The forms of assistance which are unavailable to the non-participating community include grants, loans or guarantees made by the Small Business Administration (SBA), Federal Housing Administration and the Veterans Administration. In short, no Federal assistance for acquisition or construction may be provided in flood hazard areas.

The NFIP has two levels of community eligibility, the emergency program and the regular program. To be eligible for the emergency program, a community must submit a completed application to FEMA and adopt land-use control measures consistent with FEMA regulations. The community, in its application, must document its legal authority to control land use, its efforts to reduce flood hazards, provide maps of flood-prone areas and a history of flooding in the community. The application also requires an outline of future land-use regulatory measures to be taken in compliance with FEMA requirements.

Once a community has entered the emergency program and a Flood Hazard Boundary Map identifying those areas of the community which are flood hazardous has been drawn, FEMA undertakes detailed studies to determine actuarial rates. These studies provide technical information (topographical and hydrological) which is used to prepare a flood insurance report for the community. The community is allotted a period of time to contest and appeal the findings of the report after which a Flood Insurance Rate Map is published which identifies the hazardous areas and divides the mapped area into zones according to flood hazard factors. The results of these studies translate flood frequency information into insurance rates. A community enters the regular program when the rate map has been completed. To remain in the regular program, all new or substantially improved residential structures must have their lowest floor, including basement elevated to or above the level of the 100 year flood. New or substantially improved non-residential structures must also be floodproofed to or above the 100 year flood level.

After a community qualifies for the sale of flood insurance, policies may be purchased from any licensed property insurance agent or broker. The lender typically informs the buyer or builder of a building that the property is in a special flood hazard area and that flood insurance must be purchased. The insurance agent completes the necessary forms and submits the application and full premium to the NFIP. Both building and contents may be insured; residential buildings and contents for up to $250,000 and $60,000 respectively and small business buildings and contents up to $250,000 and $300,000 respectively. In addition to residential and commercial buildings, mobile homes may also be covered. Property considered not insurable by the NFIP includes gas and liquid storage tanks, wharves, piers, bulkheads, growing crops, livestock, roads, machinery or equipment stored in the open and motor vehicles.

The NFIP requires participating communities to engage in land-use planning and hazard mitigation. With Federal Government oversight, these measures are carried out according to uniform requirements. By contrast, earthquake planning and hazard reduction are for the most part, sporadic, piecemeal and uneven local efforts. Tying the provision of subsidized flood insurance to Federal or federally-related financial assistance serves to overcome two serious problems which prevented the adequate provision of flood insurance by the private sector: the inability to adequately spread the risk (adverse selection) and a questionable ability to meet the payout requirements for PML occurrences (capacity). Prior to Federal involvement in the provision of flood insurance there existed a virtually uninsurable situation. Since flood damage is confined to relatively concentrated areas, it generated limited demand and only from those in the highest risk zones, hence the problem of adverse selection. The staggering losses caused by floods also threatened to strain the industry's capacity to meet the enormous payouts for the worst occurrences. It will be recalled that adverse selection and capacity are two of the most critical problems which currently face the insurance industry in providing earthquake coverage. A federally initiated catastrophe insurance program modeled closely on the NFIP (i.e. which was administered by FEMA, identified earthquake prone communities, set insurance rates and policy terms, subsidized premiums and provided reinsurance, enforced standards of land-use management and earthquake hazard mitigation and tied community eligibility for most disaster assistance to participation) would address most of the major problems which now restrict insurance availability.

The strategy of direct Federal intervention in the insurance market as outlined above would, in all probability, face major opposition from the insurance industry. Aside from a "free-enterprise" philosophy which regards any Federal incursion into the private marketplace with suspicion, there are other more programmatically specific concerns. The NFIP was originally touted as a joint public-private sector effort to solve a difficult national dilemma. Until the end of 1977, the National Flood Insurers Association, an organization which represented 130 of the nation's major property and casualty insurance companies monitored the writing of flood insurance and jointly administered the NFIP with FEMA. However, problems regarding the division of authority, responsibility and participation led to controversy and ultimate dissolution of the industry-government partnership. Industry officials have expressed the fear that a partnership to provide earthquake or catastrophe coverage would eventually lead to a government takeover of the program. Fears have also been expressed that a Federal program of earthquake or catastrophe insurance with mandatory participation would have a spillover effect and cause capacity problems in other non-federally insured lines (e.g. if the earthquake caused fire, what impact would the Federal program have on fire insurance?). As an indicator of stakeholder support, the Federal role "as direct provider of earthquake insurance to prospective purchasers" (Atkisson, et al., 1980: 48) received few endorsements from participants in the Earthquake Insurance Issues Workshop and was ranked a distant tenth.

There appears to be little, if any, support within the Executive Branch or Congress for a greatly expanded government role in catastrophe insurance. Consistent with the current Administration's philosophy of minimal incursion by government into the private sector, the FIA has taken the position that the Federal Government will not expand its role in the insurance industry and will seek to return the flood insurance program to industry control as soon as the program is self-supporting. There is currently no state advocacy for Federal insurance involvement in what is generally regarded as a state regulatory function.

C. Intervention to Assist the Insurance Industry in Providing More Thorough Coverage

Thus far, we have outlined two broad strategies which would address the problems of managing earthquake induced losses including the adequate provision of earthquake insurance. One strategy called for modifications in the current system of Federal disaster relief and hazard abatement, promotion and implementation of research and technical assistance but no Federal intervention as direct provider of earthquake insurance. This strategy appears to have considerable support among stakeholders but only weakly addresses the major problems confronting adequate earthquake insurance provision. A second strategy called for a comprehensive Federal insurance program wherein rates, premiums and terms of coverage would be established by the government which would also administer the program and provide reinsurance. This strategy addressed nearly all the basic problems of loss management and insurance provision but would most likely arouse vehement opposition from the insurance industry and probably in Congress and the Administration as well.

A third alternative strategy represents middle ground between government non-intervention in the private insurance market and a Federal role as provider of earthquake insurance. This strategy might be described as an attempt to assist the insurance industry in extending earthquake insurance coverage to greater numbers of consumers under essentially free market conditions. A number of actions could be taken in pursuit of this strategy. The Federal Government could act as reinsurer, either routinely or as reinsurer of last resort. It could redesign IRS policies to permit long term catastrophe reserving. A Federal catastrophe loan program could be designed to aid the insurance industry. The government could establish a cooperative reserve pool, possibly through property tax revenues. These alternatives were all mentioned at the Earthquake Insurance Issues Workshop. Those which were ranked highest by participants included the Federal role of reinsurer and provider of catastrophe loans to insurers (ranked 2nd) and government action to modify IRS policies which restrict the buildup of catastrophe reserves (ranked 5th).

These three strategic elements, provision of reinsurance, catastrophe loans to insurers and modification of IRS restraints on reserving could produce a substantial deepening of insurance industry capacity both to provide more extensive earthquake coverage and meet the payout requirements of PML events. While the reinsurance component requires Federal involvement in the insurance market it does not place the Federal Government in a position of primary provider, competitor, or exclusive source of earthquake insurance. There are two proposals generated from within the insurance industry which are designed to promote more extensive earthquake coverage while incorporating a Federal role which does not heavily impact free market conditions.

American International Group (AIG) has proposed the creation of a Federal Insurance Corporation which would sell excess catastrophe reinsurance to the insurance and reinsurance industries. (Catastrophe reinsurance calls for the primary insurer, the ceding company, to assume all loss in a catastrophe up to a specified amount beyond which the reinsurer assumes responsibility). According to the AIG proposal, the Federal reinsurance agency would not compete with the private insurance or reinsurance industries. Rather, it would provide a layer of catastrophe reinsurance in excess of the amount that can be acquired in the private reinsurance market. The program would be prefunded from premiums of insurers and reinsurers who purchase this additional earthquake protection.

21

The price charged for this reinsurance coverage would be determined in a business-like way on the same basis as occurs in determining price with a private insurer. The program, according to AIG spokesmen, would substantially increase the capacity of the insurance industry to provide catastrophe coverage. It would also help prevent insolvencies, avoid adverse selection and extensive Federal involvement in the insurance industry. A second proposal advanced by the Reinsurance Association of America recommends creation of a standby Federal Catastrophe Loan Plan. Activation of the Plan following a catastrophe would occur upon designation by FEMA and determination that catastrophe losses exceeded 20 percent of industry-wide property insurance premiums received the previous year (the 1982 figure was $8.7 billion). Insurers experiencing a surplus loss in excess of 25 percent would be eligible to borrow up to 95 percent of the surplus loss in excess of the 25 percent threshold. Loans would be repaid over a 20 year period at an interest rate comparable to U.S. obligations of similar maturity. Its backers suggest that the problems of capacity and subsequent insolvencies could be effectively addressed if the plan was adopted. The plan would require no new Federal agencies nor would it require the accumulation of a large fund. The difficulty of determining rates and premiums would be avoided since the plan is based on loans, not insurance.

The two proposals outlined clearly address the basic issue of insurance industry capacity to make large payouts for devastating events. This increased capacity, obtained by adding a layer of reinsurance and a standby loan program, would represent a significant step toward expanding earthquake coverage and avoiding insolvencies. By orienting these programs to catastrophe rather than earthquake disaster alone, the problem of adverse selection or risk spreading is also effectively addressed. This strategy, which avoids the more heavy-handed Federal roles while providing backup assistance to private insurance provision is less likely to generate industry opposition. One must question, however, the extent to which either of these plans stimulate demand for catastrophe coverage beyond present levels. The implicit assumption on the part of industry sponsors seems to be that increased risk spreading and capacity would stimulate more aggressive marketing which, along with more attractive rates, would generate enhanced demand. The NFIP, when first launched in 1968, offered subsidized insurance on a voluntary basis with negligible results in terms of purchaser interest. These plans do not incorporate incentives for communities to engage in preparedness, hazard mitigation and land-use regulation.

IV. Conclusions and Policy Recommendations

This report has traced the origin and outlined the current status of earthquake insurance (Section I), discussed the principal issues involving both purchasers and providers of earthquake insurance (Section II), and evaluated three general strategies to address the problems of adequate earthquake coverage (Section III). Our analysis and treatment of earthquake insurance as a serious public policy dilemma is grounded in physical and social science research which has produced a number of alarming findings. These findings center on the fact that Southern California (as well as other seismically active parts of the country) faces the continuing threat of a massive earthquake, one which could exceed 8 on the Richter Scale, cause billions in property damage and claim thousands of lives. Further, earthquake insurance, which could assume a key role in preparation for and recovery from such a quake, is not currently playing an optimum role. Despite its potential of spreading the risk of earthquake losses among millions of property owners, earthquake insurance is neither promoted by the insurance industry nor demanded by potential purchasers. This dilemma demands a solution if the nation is to avoid a serious economic crisis, a solution which will most likely require a Federal Government initiative. Our goal in this final section is not, however, to outline a total solution to the earthquake insurance dilemma but to offer initial steps toward addressing the issue. This goal will be accomplished by briefly summarizing our findings and offering policy recommendations. These recommendations will be organized on the basis of issues as they apply to the basic stakeholder groups. These groups will be subsumed under the categories of purchasers (homeowners, businesses and local governments) and providers (the insurance industry and the Federal Government).

A. Purchasers

1. Homeowners

Homeowners are the least likely among potential earthquake insurance purchasers to acquire coverage for their property. Events which could cause severe losses to property but have a low probability of occurrence are simply not salient to most property owners. Further, earthquakes which cause extensive property damage are rare so most people, even those residing in areas of high seismicity, will not have experienced a damaging event. Many homeowners view insurance as an investment rather than a protective mechanism so the expense of earthquake coverage may appear excessive in view of the low probability of "cashing in" on the policy. Some homeowners have misconceptions about earthquake insurance which militate against purchase, e.g. that their homeowners policies automatically cover earthquakes, that earthquake insurance is not available at all or that loans and disaster relief will be sufficient to meet their needs,

The unattractiveness of earthquake insurance to homeowners may, to some limited extent, be explained by the low probability that residential property will suffer severe damage. Statistics compiled after several major earthquakes indicate that most residential losses occur in the minimum damage percentage range. A great majority of residential structures in seismically active regions are of wood frame construction, the most earthquake resistant type. While "soft market" conditions in the insurance industry have increased the availability and affordability of earthquake insurance for some potential purchasers, there is little evidence that these conditions have resulted in greater demand for coverage among homeowners.

The basic issues to be addressed in our policy alternatives and recommendations for homeowners are availability of earthquake insurance and the stimulation of demand among this class of purchasers. A range of policy alternatives might be considered.

(1) The insurance industry and government agencies could choose to do nothing to make earthquake insurance more available to homeowners or stimulate demand among this class of purchasers. The expense required to aggressively market such coverage, the lack of public support for mandated programs and the relative earthquake resistance of most residential property might be cited to rationalize such a stance.

(2) Homeowner awareness of the earthquake threat and demand for earthquake insurance might be stimulated by a concentrated public information campaign. While such campaigns have had little impact on purchase patterns in the past, a coordinated effort to promote the sale of earthquake insurance by appropriate government agencies, the insurance industry and the media may result in greater homeowner interest.

(3) The individual insurance agent could play a greater role in generating interest in earthquake coverage if given proper incentives. Commissions are currently based on an amount proportional to the total premium which, in the case of earthquake insurance, is quite small. If commissions were raised, the agent might be willing to invest more time, make more contacts and expend greater effort to convince homeowners of the attractiveness of such coverage.

(4) Insurance companies could make earthquake insurance more attractive to homeowners by lowering rates and/or deductibles. Companies might follow the lead of some independent agents and brokers who are currently offering coverage with a $1,000 deductible rather than the prevailing 5 percent deductible.

(5) Homeowner purchase of earthquake insurance might be stimulated by mandated disclosure of hazards upon sale of property. In California, an amendment to the Alquist-Priolo Special Studies Zone Act requires that prospective buyers of property within the surface fault rupture zone be informed of this potential hazard.

(6) Financial institutions, to protect their own investments, might require earthquake coverage as a condition for new mortgage loans on residential property. Such added protection could be included as part of a comprehensive homeowner's policy for new residents of hazard-prone areas.

(7) Homeowners, either individually or as communities located in hazard-prone areas, could be required to purchase earthquake insurance as a condition for participation in a federally subsidized program of earthquake or catastrophe insurance. An application of the NFIP guidelines to earthquakes might also make certain forms of Federal disaster assistance contingent upon participation in the insurance program.

Policy Recommendation—In choosing among alternatives, policy makers must remain aware that failure to expand earthquake coverage to a much greater number of homeowners will result in extensive hazard exposure and post-event Federal relief and recovery efforts of unprecedented proportions. Although potentially useful as part of a broader program, public information campaigns, hazard disclosure and individual agent promotion of earthquake insurance will not stand alone as methods of overcoming the current lack of demand. For homeowners, some strong incentives will be required to overcome the current state of disinterest and misinformation which inhibit expanded coverage. We recommend that the Federal Government, acting through the Federal Home Loan Mortgage Association and the Federal National Mortgage Association, require the purchase of earthquake insurance in hazard-prone areas as a condition for granting home mortgage loans. We also recommend that more attractive rates and deductibles be extended to homeowners, particularly those who provide evidence of home hazard mitigation. This course of action, however, will require basic changes in the provision or supply side of the earthquake insurance market to accommodate the greatly expanded demand.

2.   Businesses

Commercial firms are an extremely heterogeneous category of earthquake insurance purchasers. They vary in size, assets, insurance and risk management expertise, vulnerability of both facilities and products and perception of earthquake threat. In terms of their propensity to purchase earthquake insurance, firms range from the small family business which is no more likely to be insured for earthquakes than the typical homeowner to the multinational corporation which has sophisticated risk management expertise and is the most likely of any class of purchasers to have earthquake insurance. Thus, with commercial coverage varying from approximately 5 to 50 percent depending on the factors listed above, demand is still an issue. This is particularly so in view of the fact that commercial and industrial property damage from earthquakes falls disproportionately in the high damage percentage range.

Large firms have a number of advantages over smaller businesses and homeowners in the earthquake insurance marketplace. Most large firms have professional risk managers whose functions include the acquisition of insurance. Most risk managers are highly aware of environmental hazards and sophisticated insurance purchasers. They are likely to view insurance not as an investment but a protective mechanism, to carefully weigh the costs and benefits of coverage, and negotiate the premium rates with insurance companies or brokers. Large firms also have the option to self-insure rather than purchase policies from insurance companies.

Small businesses are perhaps the hardest hit by earthquake losses in that there is more property at risk than in the typical residence and, in comparison with large firms, a lower profit margin from which to pay earthquake insurance premiums. They also lack sophistication regarding risk management and insurance. Unlike homeowners, business people, especially small business owners, must confront the prospect of indirect losses in the form of business disruption, loss of income and possible insolvency.

The issue which appears most salient for businesses is the stimulation of demand for and adequate provision of earthquake insurance, particularly in view of current soft market conditions in insurance and the prospect of heavy direct and indirect losses among commercial firms. The following alternatives might be considered.

(1) As for homeowners, the alternatives open to the insurance industry and government agencies to promote greater coverage among small business owners include a range of actions from maintaining the status quo to a Federal program which requires earthquake insurance.

25

(2)   Large corporations and mid-sized companies, particularly those which have not purchased commercial insurance or are now self-insured, might consider taking advantage of "soft market" conditions in insurance which have produced, in many cases, drastically reduced premiums to large corporate customers.

(3)   Large corporations, both those which have purchased insurance and those which have not, should be aware that business disruption losses may run three to ten times the direct loss to structures and merchandise. Earthquake insurance is available commercially for indirect losses and should be seriously considered.

Policy Recommendation—Small business owners face the prospect of heavy direct and indirect earthquake losses largely without the benefit of insurance. As with homeowners, business loans should be contingent upon purchase of earthquake insurance. Federal subsidies, tax credits or grants possibly administered through the SBA should be available as incentives to acquire adequate coverage. The rapid growth of risk management expertise among large and mid-sized firms, combined with current attractive insurance rates for corporate purchasers, are likely to mean a continued trend toward greater insurance coverage among this class of purchasers. Special incentives and programs for earthquake insurance purchase among large firms are probably unnecessary at this time.

3.   Local Governments

A number of parallels between business and government with regard to earthquake losses and insurance are evident. Risk management is playing an increasingly important role in public, as well as corporate administration. Government jurisdictions, like businesses, face the prospect of heavy indirect losses in an earthquake disaster. For local government, these indirect losses take the form of tax and service interruption and potential liability. Direct losses suffered by both local governments and commercial firms tend to occur in the high damage percentage range. Large local governments may opt to self-insure rather than purchase coverage commercially. By contrast, small local jurisdictions, to the extent that they purchase earthquake insurance at all, seek coverage commercially, sometimes jointly in insurance pooling arrangements. Self-insurance, which is also an option for large corporations, involves a deliberate retention of financial responsibility for earthquake induced losses to public facilities and various indirect losses as well. The resources tapped for recovery under a program of self-insurance may include general revenue or revenue increases, diversion of funds from existing programs, accumulated catastrophe reserves and Federal disaster assistance.

While most government units are large enough to benefit from a buyer's insurance market (recall that a soft insurance market has meant lower premiums for large purchasers), reduction of earthquake hazards has been relegated to the bottom of most public policy agendas. Thus, while many local governments have risk management functionaries who are aware of earthquake hazards and encourage the purchase of insurance, legislative or administrative action to approve the acquisition of coverage may not be forthcoming. Even if environmental hazards are deemed a serious enough threat to warrant action, earthquake insurance may be passed over in favor of life saving mitigation measures, e.g. retrofitting or razing unreinforced masonry buildings.

The major issues among local governments, then, are whether to insure, how to insure and the priority placed on earthquake insurance among other public policy matters. These issues can be elaborated as several policy alternatives.

(1)   A local government may remain uninsured for earthquake losses and respond to matters higher on the public policy agenda.

(2)   Local jurisdictions may invest limited public funds for natural hazard reduction in preparedness, earthquake hazard mitigation or emergency response rather than purchase earthquake insurance.

(3)   Local governments, particularly large jurisdictions, can purchase earthquake insurance at attractive rates due to the soft market for insurance which currently prevails.

(4)   Small governments can also take advantage of lower earthquake insurance premiums by forming pooling arrangements with other jurisdictions.

(5)   An alternative to commercially purchased coverage is self-insurance which ideally would contain the following elements: a thorough knowledge of what facilities are at risk; a program of risk reduction which includes land-use planning, preparedness and earthquake hazard mitigation; a plan which identifies revenue sources, program funds and reserves to be diverted for emergency response and recovery; a detailed understanding of Federal disaster assistance programs available to local government; the purchase of privately provided insurance for a level of risk beyond which a local entity cannot reasonably expect to assume responsibility; and catastrophe reserves, at least sufficient to carry a jurisdiction through the emergency period.

(6)   Local governments may purchase earthquake insurance for indirect losses, particularly tax interruption policies which guarantee a steady flow of revenue should an earthquake destroy principal revenue sources. This alternative is relevant mainly to small local governments whose principal revenue source(s) is comprised of one or a few facilities (e.g. a shopping center or central business district).

Policy Recommendations—Earthquake insurance is currently available to local governments at attractive rates. Small jurisdictions should form pooling arrangements to take advantage of lower premiums available to large purchasers. We strongly recommend that small jurisdictions purchase tax interruption coverage to assure a continued flow of revenue in the event that primary tax sources are lost. Such a steady flow of income will be of critical importance for a rapid recovery. Self-insurance is a viable alternative to commercially acquired coverage for large local governments whose premiums would be enormous even with good rates and low premiums. Self-insurance, however, must be part of an overall program of risk management. Our research has revealed that many self-insured jurisdictions do not have an accurate and updated inventory of their hazard exposed facilities. They have not identified specific sources of relief and recovery funds to be diverted for an emergency from their current budgets, and they have only a cursory knowledge of Federal disaster assistance programs and eligibility requirements. Further, self-insured local governments tend to retain more financial responsibility for potential earthquake damage than they have the capacity to adequately cover themselves. Supplemental private earthquake insurance should be acquired to reduce the burden of risk retention. We urge those governments which self-insure to bring their programs into line with the general criteria outlined in policy alternative 5. While we strongly recommend that earthquake insurance purchase be a high priority budget item for local governments in seismically hazardous areas, we realize that risk reduction measures which are designed to save lives are of greater urgency and must take precedence over the protection of property.

B. Providers

Nearly all of the policy recommendations made in the previous section would serve to increase the demand for commercially marketed earthquake insurance. But in the absence of fundamental changes in the present system of insurance provision, this greatly expanded demand could not be effectively satisfied. We have outlined these problems with provision as: actuarial and rate setting difficulties, industry capacity to meet the payout requirements resulting from PML events, IRS restraints on catastrophe reserving, adverse selection and risk spreading difficulties, ineffective loss reducing activities by local jurisdictions and difficulties in determining probable earthquake loss and the insurability of properties. These problems serve to restrict the availability of earthquake insurance in that companies, faced with uncertainty and the possibility of heavy payout requirements, refuse to provide coverage beyond certain self imposed limits. While it remains true that current economic conditions have produced a short term increase in the availability and affordability of earthquake insurance, the margin of expanded availability is small and consistent with present low levels of demand. The soft market is a somewhat fragile trend which could easily be reversed by heavy underwriting losses or a significant decline in return on insurance industry investments. The serious systemic problems outlined above must be addressed before the industry can meet the pressures of a greatly expanded demand for earthquake insurance.

Most of the provider related problems outlined above are not within the capacity of the insurance industry to resolve alone. The magnitude of the problems and the sobering consequences of not resolving them have led us to argue that some form of Federal involvement will be necessary to effectively address the dilemma.

In Section III we outlined three strategies which are available to the Federal Government in confronting the problem of earthquake losses. These strategies were assessed in terms of their feasibility, acceptability to stakeholders and their ability to address the basic issues of expanded earthquake coverage. The strategy of non-intervention into the earthquake insurance marketplace (of maintaining the status quo or modifying Federal disaster assistance policies) was popular among stakeholders, especially insurance industry representatives, but failed to address the problems of earthquake insurance provision. The strategy of direct intervention by the Federal Government to provide earthquake insurance would tackle nearly all of the difficulties with provision but would face tremendous resistance from the insurance industry and possibly other stakeholders as well. The third strategy called for Federal intervention to expand the availability of earthquake insurance under essentially free market conditions. Since most policy alternatives consistent with these strategies were discussed in Section III, we will move directly to policy recommendations.

Policy Recommendations—Because of its potential effectiveness in averting market failure, we endorse the concept of all-catastrophe insurance mandated by the Federal Government and administered through a corporate body made up of public and private representatives as a long-term goal. However, we regard the most acceptable, feasible and effective short-term strategy open to the Federal Government as one which involves actions designed to facilitate expanded earthquake insurance coverage without direct intervention as an insurance provider. We recommend careful consideration by Congress and the Administration of two proposals outlined in Section III; one would create a Federal Insurance Corporation to sell excess catastrophe reinsurance to the insurance and reinsurance industries, the other would establish a standby Federal Catastrophe Loan Plan. These programs, advanced by members of the insurance industry, would serve to extend capacity, avoid adverse selection and prevent individual insurance company insolvencies. While these plans do call for a Federal role in expanding earthquake insurance availability, they do not place the government in the position of primary insurance provider or competitor with the private sector. The Federal Insurance Corporation would provide a layer of catastrophe reinsurance in excess of the amount that can be acquired in the private reinsurance market. The Federal Catastrophe Loan Plan would take effect only if insurance industry reserves were depleted beyond a threshold level. We also find merit in a proposal that IRS restrictions on the buildup of catastrophe reserves be modified to facilitate reserving. This too would expand the insurance industry's capacity to meet the payout demands of PML events. In conjunction with the programs outlined above, the ability to increase catastrophe reserves would contribute to expanded earthquake insurance availability.

There are other problems in providing expanded insurance coverage some of which are now being addressed. The accurate determination of probable earthquake loss has been the focus of a series of reports by the California Department of Insurance. These reports, titled, *California Earthquake Zoning and Probable Maximum Loss Evaluation Program*, represent significant advances in data collection on zone exposures in terms of the impact of PML events. This effort should receive continued support and similar evaluation programs in other earthquake hazard-prone states should be initiated. Another problem has been identified as ineffective loss reducing activities by local jurisdictions affecting the insurability of property. We recommend that insurance companies offer incentives in the form of rebates or premium reductions for individuals, firms or local jurisdictions which provide evidence of hazard mitigation efforts, preparedness, and land-use regulation. These incentives should be backed up by Federal Government loans and grants-in-aid for loss reduction measures. Actuarial and rate setting problems are often mentioned by earthquake insurance stakeholders as an impediment to the expanded provision of coverage but calculation of more accurate rates faces formidable obstacles. The infrequency of earthquakes, changing demographic and development patterns and programmatic changes within the insurance industry contribute to a rate structure based more on guesswork than a firmly established database. Some experimentation has been done with new techniques of computing earthquake insurance rates using simulation models. Such research should continue to be backed by funding from the insurance industry and the Federal Government.

Appendix A

California Earthquake Premiums

1977-1982

1977	19,795.536	1980	38,540.205
1978	23,158.724	1981	50,207.836
1979	28,968.085	1982	58,877.353

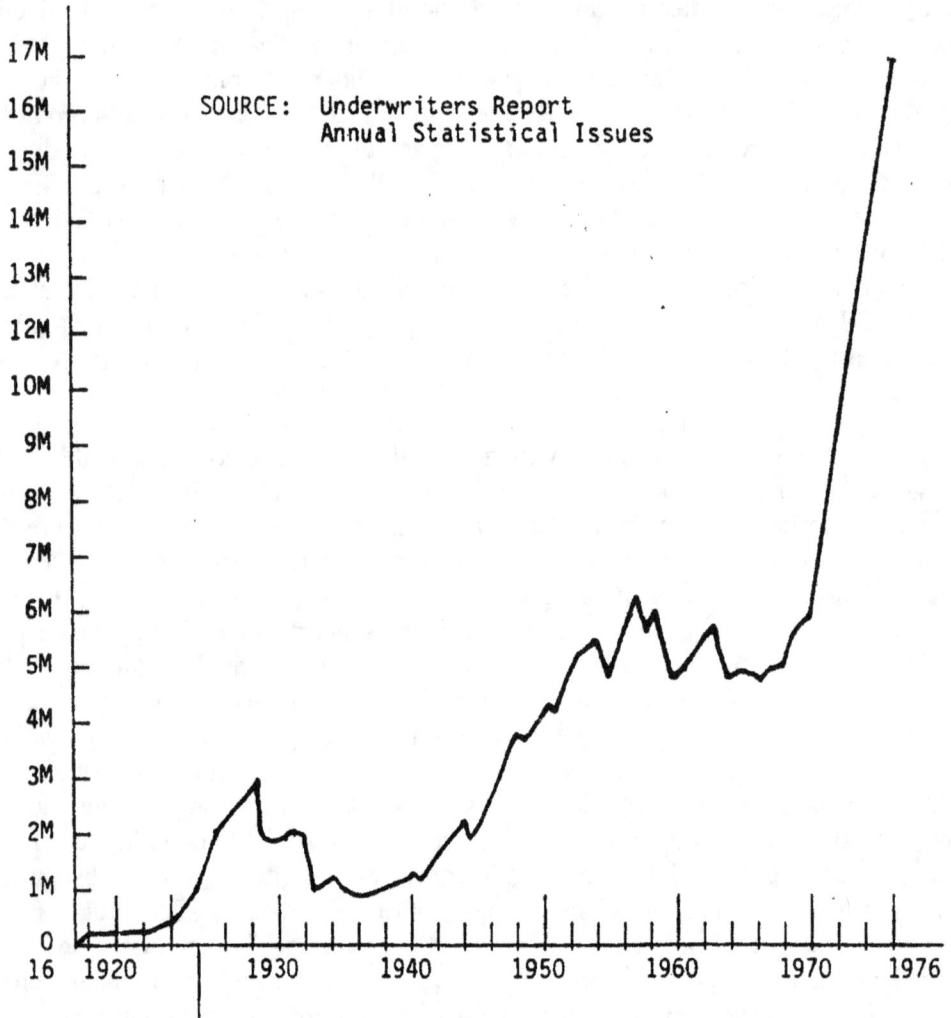

SOURCE: Underwriters Report
Annual Statistical Issues

1925 - Santa Barbara Earthquake

SOURCE: Steinbrugge (Updated)

California Earthquake Insurance Program (1916-1982)

Appendix B

Interview Schedule for Risk Managers
SCEPP Earthquake Insurance Study

1. **Demographics**
   a. Identification Code for jurisdiction
   b. Jurisdiction size (population, assets, resources)
   c. Type of administration
   d. Position of person interviewed (Risk Manager, Administrative Officer, etc.)

2. **What types of insurance coverages does the jurisdiction carry?**

3. **Does the jurisdiction have earthquake insurance?**

4. **Since cities and other jurisdictions are eligible for Federal disaster relief, what relief aid do you expect from the government and what must you provide for yourselves?**

5. How was it decided that earthquake insurance should be carried by the jurisdiction?
   a. What forces supported it?
   b. What forces opposed it?
   c. What were the arguments on either side?
   d. Once initiated, who took action to establish coverage?

6. **Is earthquake coverage purchased from a private insurance company or is the jurisdiction self-insured?**

   If coverage is purchased from a private insurance firm, answer 7-10.

7. **Why did the jurisdiction purchase insurance from a private firm rather than self-insure?**

8. **How was a firm chosen?**

9. **What is insured? And how was it determined that these facilities or exposures should be insured?**

10. **What type of earthquake insurance policy was purchased and what are the terms?**
    a. Total coverage held
    b. Rate
    c. Deductible
    d. Coverage on value of property or replacement cost
    e. Ratio of coverage for direct vs. indirect losses

11. **Why did the jurisdiction self-insure rather than approach a private insurance firm?**

12. **How does the plan work?**
    a. What are the sources of funding for the plan?
    b. What facilities or exposures come under the plan?
    c. Are there funds held in reserve in the event of a catastrophic event? How much?
    d. Are there risk pooling arrangements with other cities or governmental units?

13. **Does the plan call for both self-insurance and privately acquired coverage?**
    a. What is covered by each plan?
    b. Why did the jurisdiction self-insure for part of the risk and acquire private coverage for other exposures?

14. **Have you given any thought to insurance coverage against losses or liability resulting from response to a credible earthquake prediction?**

Appendix C

Aggregated Nominal Group View of Federal Role in Managing Earthquake-Induced Losses

Recommended Federal Role	No. votes cast for indicated answers	Aggregate point value of votes
1. Stimulate and support improved use and enforcement of earthquake loss-mitigating measures, including construction and land-use standards, by state and local governments.	36	109
2. Act as reinsurer, either routinely or as insurer of last resort, and/or provide "catastrophe" loans to insurers.	28	90
3. Revise current disaster relief and tax policies/programs so as to stimulate both increased purchase of earthquake insurance and use of loss-reducing mitigations.	16	54
4. Implement expanded Federal program of research, technical assistance, and risk mapping in support of operations by state/local governments and private industry.	20	53
5. Modify IRS policies so as to permit long-term catastrophe reserving.	16	47
6. Do nothing more. Maintain existing system. Adopt policy of not mandating coverage and/or not intruding further into the current insurance system.	12	44
7. Require recipients of federally backed loans to purchase earthquake insurance.	6	22
8. Improve Federal policy-making and management operations targeted on earthquake response, mitigation, and insurance activities through such means as: (1) prioritizing importance of earthquake programs relative to other social needs; (2) moving slowly and deliberately in changing existing policies/programs; (3) establishing and maintaining a "stable system of rules"; (4) promoting the development of earthquake prediction and response plans at all levels of government; (5) conducting a study of the economic impacts on long-term financial markets that might be produced by an expanded government role in earthquake insurance.	6	17
9. Require inclusion of hazard zone notifications in title insurance policies and/or in other communications to property purchasers at time of title transfer.	5	7
10. Act as direct provider of earthquake insurance to prospective purchasers.	4	7
11. Sponsor program of public education on earthquake risks, mitigation, response, and/or insurance.	3	7
12. Limit the financial liability of private insurance carriers and their risk of PML-induced insolvency through such means as legally specifying the maximum intensity quake for which varying fractions of claims must be honored.	2	5
13. Encourage free market purchase of insurance.	1	4
14. Levy surcharge on all insurance policies so as to provide coverage against all catastrophes.	1	3
15. Guarantee availability of insurance, if earthquake insurance is mandated.	1	3
16. Provide funds to states with "high priority needs" in order to finance efforts to prevent failure of dams.	1	3

Source: Atkisson, Petak and Anderson

References

Algermissen, S.T., Reinhart, W.A., and Dewey, J.
   1977   A Study of Earthquake Losses in The San Francisco Bay Area: Data and Analysis.
          Washington, D. C., U. S. Department of Commerce

Anderson, D., Petak, W. J. and Widell, C. E.
   1981   Earthquake Insurance Practices, Technical Report No. 1388-2, Redondo Beach,
          CA: J. H. Wiggins Company

Atkisson, A. A., Petak, W. J. Anderson, D. R.
   1980   Earthquake Insurance Issues Workshop: Problems and Issues Associated With Use
          of Insurance Systems to Mitigate the Impact of Future Earthquake Losses Within
          the U.S. Redondo Beach, CA: J. H. Wiggins and Company.

Atkisson, A. A. and Petak, W. J.
   1981   Earthquake Insurance: A Public Policy Analysis Technical Report No. 1388-4.
          Redondo Beach, CA: J. H. Wiggins and Company.

California Department of Insurance
   1983   California Earthquake Zoning and Probable Maximum Loss Evaluation Program,
          Sacramento, California.

Delbecq, A. L., Van de Ven, A. H. and Gustafson, 0. H.
   1975   Group Techniques for Program Planning: A Guide for Nominal Group and Delphi
          Processes, Glenview, Illinois: Scott, Freeman and Company.

Driver, R.F. and Company
   1983   Earthquake defined for insurance policy written for Orange County Cities Risk
          Management Authority. Newport Beach, CA

Hudson, J.M. and Petak, W. J,
   1981   "How Earthquake Coverage Shakes Out Across the U.S." Risk Management,
          October, 1981.

Kunrether, H.
   1978   Disaster Insurance Protection: Public Policy Lessons. New York: John Wiley and
          Sons

Kunrether, H.
   1980   "Issues on Earthquake Insurance: A Position Paper" (Prepared for the J.H. Wiggins
          Company, Redondo Beach, CA)

Los Angeles Department of Building and Safety
   1971   "Los Angeles City Damage, San Fernando Earthquake"

National Security Council and the Federal Emergency Management Agency
   1980   "An Assessment of The Consequences and Preparations for a Catastrophic
          California Earthquake: Findings and Actions Taken" Washington, D. C.

Olson, M. J.
 1971   The Logic of Collective Action: Public Goods and the Theory of Groups. New
        York, Schocken Books.

Steinbrugge, Karl
 1982   Earthquakes, Volcanoes, Tsunamis: An Anatomy of Hazards. New York, Scandia
        America Group.

U. S. Department of Commerce
 1969   Studies in Seismicity and Earthquake Damage Statistics. Washington, D.C.

www.ingramcontent.com/pod-product-compliance
Lightning Source LLC
Chambersburg PA
CBHW080614290526
45790CB00007B/2775